Meg and Greg

A Handful of Dogs

Meg and Greg

A Handful of Dogs

with

and more consonant suffixes **-s**

-ing and more vowel suffixes

-ed a suffix said three ways

ex- and more prefixes

Four Phonics Stories

Written by
Elspeth Rae and Rowena Rae

Illustrated by
Elisa Gutiérrez

ORCA BOOK PUBLISHERS

Published in Canada and the United States in 2024 by Orca Book Publishers.
orcabook.com

Library and Archives Canada Cataloguing in Publication
Title: A handful of dogs : with four phonics stories / written by Elspeth Rae and Rowena Rae ;
illustrated by Elisa Gutiérrez.Names: Rae, Elspeth, 1973- author. | Rae, Rowena, author. |
Gutiérrez, Elisa, 1972- illustrator. Series: Rae, Elspeth, 1973- Meg and Greg ; 5.
Description: Series statement: Meg and Greg ; 5 | Practices the sounds s, ing, ed, and ex.
Identifiers: Canadiana (print) 20230567061 | Canadiana (ebook) 2023056707x |
ISBN 9781459838239 (softcover) | ISBN 9781459838246 (PDF) | ISBN 9781459838253 (EPUB)
Subjects: LCSH: Reading—Phonetic method—Problems, exercises, etc. |
LCSH: Reading—Phonetic method—
Study and teaching (Elementary) | LCGFT: Short stories. | LCGFT: Problems and exercises.
Classification: LCC PS8635.A39 H36 2024 | DDC jC813/.6—dc23

Library of Congress Control Number: 2023946689

Summary: In the fifth book in the phonics-based, decodable Meg and Greg series,
Meg and Greg are back at school for new adventures with friends in four stories that
introduce readers to suffixes and prefixes. Includes illustrations and worksheets.

Orca Book Publishers is committed to reducing the consumption of
nonrenewable resources in the production of our books. We make every
effort to use materials that support a sustainable future.

Orca Book Publishers gratefully acknowledges the support for its publishing programs provided
by the following agencies: the Government of Canada, the Canada Council for the Arts and the
Province of British Columbia through the BC Arts Council and the Book Publishing Tax Credit.

Series design and illustration by Elisa Gutiérrez.
Edited by Vanessa McCumber.

Printed and bound in Canada.

27 26 25 24 • 1 2 3 4

For all young readers who are
learning to crack the code!
—E.R. and R.R.

To neurodivergent
individuals and their families.
"In diversity there is beauty
and there is strength."
(Maya Angelou)
—E.G.

In this book:

consonant suffixes
-ful -ly
-ment -s

vowel suffixes
-en -er -es
-est -ing

suffix -ed
-ed

prefixes
de- dis-
ex- in- pre-
re- un-

Contents

How to read the stories in this book

Adult or buddy reader's text

Kid's text

Meg and Greg is a series of **decodable** phonics storybooks for children ages 6 to 9 who are learning to read. The stories are designed for shared reading between an experienced reader and a learning reader. This is especially helpful for children who have the added challenge of **dyslexia** or another language-based learning difficulty. A child feeling overwhelmed at reading sentences could start by reading only the illustration labels. More about this approach is on page 153.

Who are these stories decodable for?

The kid's text in this book is **decodable** by a child who knows:

- basic **consonant** sounds
- **consonant blends**
- **short vowel sounds**
- **digraphs** *ck, sh, ch, th, nk, ng*
- **trigraphs** *tch, dge*
- **magic e** *a-e, e-e, i-e, o-e, u-e*
- **r-controlled vowels** /ar/, /or/, /er/, /air/ sounds

The stories in this book focus on **suffixes** and **prefixes**:

- consonant suffixes *-ful, -ly, -ment, -s*
- vowel suffixes *-en, -er, -es, -est, -ing, -y*
- vowel suffix *-ed*
- prefixes *de-, dis-, ex-, in-, pre-, re-, un-*

A note about suffixes

Adding a suffix to a word sometimes means adjusting the **base word**. For example, sometimes we drop a silent *e*, or double the final consonant, or change the letter *y* to an *i* before adding the suffix. Children must learn the rules to make these adjustments before they can read this book. More about these rules on pages 150–152.

Warning!

These little words can be tricky to read.

a, as, has, is, his

of, the, do, to, I

be, he, me, she, we

OK, have, give, you

"all" family
(ball, small, etc.)

what, when, where, which, why

was, go, no, so

New for this book

by, my

here

said

they

your

Find out more about these tricky words on page 148.

All the stories
in this book introduce words
that have a **suffix** or a **prefix**.
This story focuses on words with
suffixes that begin with a **consonant**.
The suffixes we include are *-ful*, *-ly*,
-ment and *-s*. There are other consonant
suffixes, such as *-less* and *-ness*, that we
haven't included. To build their vocabulary,
it's helpful for children to know the
meanings of the suffixes in this story:
-ful means "full of" (*helpful*).
-ly means "in the manner of" (*sadly*).
-ment means "the result of an action"
(*development*).
-s means "more than one of" (*cats*),
"belonging to" (*Greg's dog*) or "what
someone or something (he, she or it) is doing
in present tense" (*he runs*).
For a list of consonant suffix words,
including all the ones used in this story,
go to megandgregbooks.com.

A Handful of Dogs

A story featuring consonant suffixes

-ful, -ly, -ment, -s

dog snacks

Chapter 1

A **Stressful** Start

Meg and Greg dashed into their classroom
just as their teacher clapped her **hands** to
get **everyone's** attention.

"OK, fifth **graders!**" Miss Lin said
cheerfully. "Our **school's** Fall Fair fundraiser
is tomorrow. Let's go over all the **stations**
and make sure everyone **knows** their job."

A murmur of **excitement** rippled through
the room.

Miss Lin pointed at a list on the board.
"Please raise your **hands** when I call your
group's station. Bake sale. Craft table. Game
zone. Pumpkin carving. Dog obstacle course."

Greg's hand shot **quickly** into the air.

That's us! But we call it the Dog Dash!

I like that! Dog Dash. I will **gladly** update the list.

Miss Lin

Miss Lin, what time do we set up in the morning?

Meg

Set up at 9!

You can start setting up at nine. Ticket **sales** start at ten.

Miss Lin put her pen back on the desk. "Please move into your **groups**, and go over any last **tasks** you need to finish today."

Meg, Greg, Jordan and Anka pushed their **desks** together.

"Here's our checklist for the Dog Dash," Greg said. He **slowly** pulled a crumpled piece of paper from his desk.

Meg smoothed out the paper. "Dog **snacks**. I picked up a **bagful** from **Jenkin's** Pet Shop yesterday."

"Awesome!" Greg pointed to the next item on the list. "Jordan and I have most of the obstacle-course **equipment**."

dog snacks

flags

bench

tunnel

"Yup, we have **flags** and a bench for the **dogs** to run along. And we have a tunnel, but no slide," Jordan said.

"The kindergarten class will **probably** lend us a small slide," Anka said.

"OK, I can ask," Greg said.

Meg made check **marks** on the list. "Anka, did you make **ribbons** for the **winners?**"

"Yes!" Anka said.

"Perfect. We are all set," Meg said.

"This will be a blast!" Greg said.

slide

ribbons

Dog Dash!

The next morning, **Greg's** alarm rang **early**. *Buzz! Buzz!*

Greg rubbed his **eyes** and stretched **slowly**. Then he remembered the Fall Fair. "Today's the Dog Dash!" He jumped out of bed, opened the **curtains** and peered outside. "Oh no!" he cried. He ran to get his phone. Meg had already texted the group chat.

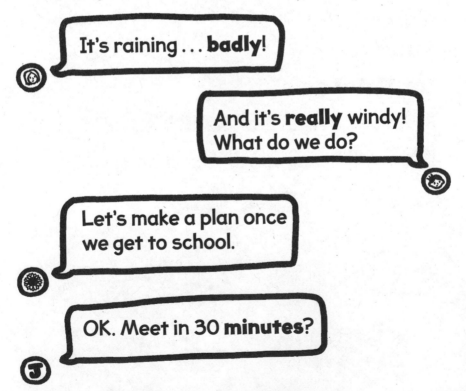

It's raining . . . **badly!**

And it's **really** windy! What do we do?

Let's make a plan once we get to school.

OK. Meet in 30 **minutes**?

Meg held a big umbrella. "**Quickly**! Under here!"

Greg, Jordan and Anka ran up.

"It's so wet! We can't run the Dog Dash in this," Greg said **sadly**.

"Let's think," Anka said. "Can we rent a tent?"

"From where?" Greg said.

Suddenly Meg lit up. "**Jenkin's** Pet Shop! They have a big tent!"

"Do you think Miss Jenkin will lend it to us?" Greg said.

"**Hopefully**!" Meg said.

umbrella

Greg

Meg

Anka

Jordan

-s . . .

Chapter 2

Suddenly ... Swish!

Meg and Greg sheltered from the rain under the awning in front of **Jenkin's** Pet Shop.

"Good thing they open at nine o'clock," Greg said. "We should have enough time to get back to school and set up the tent before people start arriving."

"**Hopefully** Miss Jenkin **agrees** to lend it to us!" Meg said.

Suddenly a light flicked on inside the shop. Meg and Greg put their **faces** to the glass. Meg tapped **lightly** to get Miss **Jenkin's** attention.

dog **bones**   **cat** litter

cat
scratch

Miss Jenkin led Meg and Greg through her pet shop and **downstairs** to the **basement**. "The tent is **fairly** big, but it's easy to put up and down."

"This tent is huge!" Meg said. "Let's each take one end."

"Don't forget these!" Miss Jenkin said. She tucked a **bagful** of tent **pegs** under **Greg's** arm.

Greg smiled. "Thank you again, Miss Jenkin. This is so **helpful**!"

Meg nodded. "This tent will work **perfectly**!"

"Jordan, Anka!" Greg said. "We got the tent! And it's *big*!"

Jordan and Anka ran to help Meg and Greg.

"**Hopefully** all the Dog Dash stuff will fit under it," Anka said.

"Let's set it up on this flat bit of grass," Jordan said.

The **kids** got the tent up. The bench, tunnel and slide fit **perfectly**. Greg set up **chairs** for the dog **parents**.

-s . . .

Jordan and Greg stood **proudly** looking at everything they had set up.

"We did it!" Greg said. "Just in time too. It's raining even harder than before!"

"Let's hang up our sign, and then we're ready," Meg said, picking up the Dog Dash banner. "Greg, could you hold that end to stop it from flapping while I tie it up?"

"Hurry. It's **nearly** ten o'clock," Jordan said. "And look, here come the first people with **dogs**."

"Welcome! Come out of the storm!" Meg called.

Rocket

Scarlet

MEGATENT

pegs

DOG DASH

chairs

"Time to start the fun!" Jordan said. "Do we have five **dogs** for the first run?"

"Yup," Greg said, getting the **dogs** into a line.

"Time to *dash!*" Anka said. She held up her hand. "On your **marks**, get set, GO!"

The **dogs** ran **quickly** along the bench. They dove into the tunnel. They ran up the slide. And **suddenly** . . .

Swish! The wind swept the tent into the air!

Chapter 3

Suddenly ... Bang!

Whoosh.

"Our tent!" Anka cried.

The tent tumbled **swiftly** across the grass. Meg, Greg and Jordan ran after it. Max, Rocket and Pip **excitedly** joined the chase. "Bark!" "Ruff!" "Yip!"

Greg was in the lead. Just as he reached for the tent, the wind picked it up again. The tent sailed over the school fence and landed with a splash in a pond.

"Darn this wind. Stop being so **unhelpful**!" Meg groaned.

The **kids** ran to the edge of the pond. "Which of us will go in to fetch it?" Jordan said.

"I will. I can **hardly** get much wetter!" Greg said.

"Pass me that corner of the tent, Greg!" Meg said.

With **lots** of tugging, Meg, Greg and Jordan got the tent back to shore.

Together everyone carried the tent back to the obstacle course. Anka and the **spectators** cheered as Meg, Greg and Jordan set the tent back in place.

Anka laughed. "Look what I found," she said, holding up the **bagful** of tent **pegs**.

pegs

"Aha! Those will be **useful**!" Meg said.

Meg, Greg and Jordan held the tent in place while Anka banged in the **pegs**.

OK, **dogs!** Time to get back to the fun and **games!**

We have five **dogs** at the starting line.

Pip

On your **marks,** get set, GO!

Scarlet

The **dogs** ran **quickly** along the bench.

They dove into the tunnel.

Smoke

Max

They ran up the slide. And **suddenly . . .**

Bang!

A clap of thunder split the air.

Chapter 4

Suddenly ... *Yip!*

The thunder boomed **sharply** again. Rocket woofed. Smoke yapped. Scarlet yelped. Pip yipped and leaped in the air. She landed on top of the tunnel, and it began to roll **slowly** out of the tent. Pip started running, and the faster she ran, the faster the tunnel rolled.

"Yip! Yip!"

Smoke **quickly** bolted out of the tent. Then Rocket rushed off. Then Scarlet scampered away.

Greg turned to the **spectators**. "Don't worry! We've got this!"

Anka promptly ran after Smoke.

Greg swiftly ran after Rocket.

Anka

Max

Jordan

Meg quickly ran after Scarlet.

Jordan rapidly ran after Pip.

Pip kept running on top of the tunnel.

Yip! Yip!

tunnel

Just as Jordan caught up with Pip, the tunnel slammed **forcefully** into the school **principal's** car. Pip flew **gracefully** over the car and soared **silently** through the air. Her coat got snagged at the top of a swing set.

"Oh no!" Jordan cried. "Greg, Meg, Anka! Come **quickly**! Pip is in trouble."

Greg, Meg and Anka turned toward **Jordan's** voice and ran to help. Jordan stood **directly** below Pip, holding out his **arms**.

swing set

Suddenly a gust of wind flung Pip back into the air.

"Yip! Yip!"

"**Quickly**! Catch her!" Meg said.

Thunk!

"Got you, Pip!" Jordan said.

Meg spoke **softly** to Pip. "You gave us a scare! Let's get you **safely** back to the tent."

"And we have to get the rest of the **dogs** back," Greg said.

"These **dogs** are a **handful**," Anka said, looking around.

"Let's split up and look for them," Greg said.

Meg found Smoke chasing **balls** in the game zone. "Come on, Smoke."

Anka heard **giggles** coming from the craft table. Two **kindergarteners** were sprinkling glitter on **Rocket's** fur.

"Please stop, **kids!**" Anka called. She brushed off **Rocket's** head.

Greg spotted **movement** inside a giant pumpkin next to the carving table. He bent to look. "There you are, Scarlet! That thunder sure scared you."

pumpkins

-s . . .

glitter

The **kids** met at the pumpkin stand.

"We have Smoke, Rocket, Scarlet and Pip. We are just missing Max," Greg said.

"Where did he go?" Meg said.

Anka lit up. "I bet he is at the bake sale tent. They have a **plateful** of dog **cupcakes** for sale!"

"Yum!" Jordan said.

"Not **exactly**! Unless you are a dog," Meg said.

"Let's go and check," Greg said.

arts and crafts

Pumpkin Stand

Suddenly ... *Burp!*

At the bake sale tent, **lots** of people were in line to buy **treats**. The four **kids** searched under the **tables** and behind the cake boxes.

"Has anyone seen a big brown dog?" Meg asked **hopefully**. Everyone shook their **heads**.

Anka frowned. "I was sure Max would be here looking for food."

Jordan stood in front of the cake tent, scanning the area for Max.

34

-s . . .

"That's him!" Jordan said. "Max is back in the Dog Dash tent."

"**Exactly** where we left him! Let's go!" Anka said.

The **kids** and **dogs** ran back to the tent.

Meg froze. "Max! What are you up to?"

Suddenly . . .

"Burp!" Max licked his **lips**. He was sitting on the table next to an empty bowl.

Anka's eyes popped in **amazement**. "Max ate all the dog **treats**!"

"Those **treats** weren't just for you," Meg said **sternly**.

Max wagged his tail **contentedly**.

"Now what will we give the **dogs** when they finish the Dog Dash?" Jordan asked.

"I have ten **dollars** in my pocket," Greg said.

"How does that help us?" Meg asked.

wag, wag

Max

We can spend the $10 on five of those dog **cupcakes**.

I get it!

Greg ran off to get the **cupcakes**.

The **kids** got the **dogs** back in line.

Hopefully this is the last time!

On your **marks**, get set, GO!

The **dogs** ran **quickly** along the bench. They dove into the tunnel. They ran up the slide. And Smoke ran across the finish line first!

The End

Turn the page for more practice with consonant suffixes!

-s . . .

consonant suffixes
word search

Find the words listed below in the puzzle.
Words are hidden ➜ and ↓

```
h  m  u  w  s  x  h  s  r  t  n  t
t  i  m  e  l  y  c  w  u  l  f  h
r  n  a  s  z  x  a  i  r  a  g  a
e  r  v  t  f  e  i  f  v  c  t  n
s  g  c  r  k  r  r  t  p  a  i  k
t  l  f  i  z  a  p  l  w  k  k  f
f  a  x  c  h  b  l  y  z  e  k  u
u  d  x  t  f  b  a  h  u  s  t  l
l  l  h  l  g  i  n  d  m  k  p  n
a  y  n  y  d  t  e  s  g  t  a  g
a  n  i  s  q  s  s  q  p  e  z  o
c  k  i  s  o  f  t  l  y  m  p  q
```

airplanes	restful	thankful
cakes	softly	timely
gladly	strictly	
rabbits	swiftly	

-s . . .

consonant suffixes
crossword

Hint: Remember that suffixes have meanings.
For more information, see page 10.

Across ➡

4. **The result of** developing is a

_____.

6. The children helped their teacher clean up. They were **full of** help.
8. **More than one** skunk.
9. **More than one** carrot.
10. Students learn to handle kitchen knives **in a way that** is safe.
11. The princess fought the dragon **in a way that** was brave.

Down ⬇

1. The reusable bag had lots of uses. It was **full of** use.
2. The dog looked out at the rain **in a way that** was glum.
3. **The result of** being amazed is

_____.

5. The boy closed the door **in a way that** was quick.
7. Some snakes have poisonous venom that is **full of** harm.

Also available at megandgregbooks.com

All the
stories in this book
introduce words that have
a **suffix** or a **prefix**.
This story focuses on words with suffixes
that begin with a vowel. The suffixes we include
in this story are *-en*, *-er*, *-es*, *-est*, *-ing* and *-y*.
We haven't included *-ed*, because we focus on
that suffix in the third story of this book. There are
other vowel suffixes, such as *-able* and *-ist*, that
we haven't included.

To build their vocabulary, it's helpful for children
to know the meanings of the suffixes in this story:

-en means "to make" (*sharpen*) or "made of"
(*wooden*).

-er means "a person who" (*baker*) or "more"
(*bigger*).

-es means "more than one" (*buses*) or "telling what
someone else is doing in present tense" (*he fixes*).

-est means "the most" (*fastest*).

-ing indicates an action (*running*) or something
related to an action (*surprising*).

-y means "full of" (*lumpy*), "small/dear" (*puppy*) or
"state of" (*happy*).

For a list of vowel suffix words, including all the
ones used in this story, go to megandgregbooks.com.

This story introduces two rules for adding
suffixes: (1) the 1–1–1 Doubling Rule (*redden,
runner, flattest, jogging, funny*) and (2) the
Final *e* Rule (*ripen, baker, safest, timing,
bony*). See pages 150–151 for
information on how these
rules work.

The Amazing Quest

A story featuring vowel suffixes

-en, -er, -es, -est, -ing, -y

Teddy

skipping ropes

Chapter 1

Starting the Quest

Meg knocked on Greg's front door.

"**Coming**!" Greg yelled, **leaning** out the window.

Meg sat down to wait on the doorstep. Greg flung the door open and nearly fell over Meg.

"Let's go! Today's **going** to be **amazing**!" Greg said, **running** past Meg.

"Slow down, Greg! Miss Lin hasn't even told us what today's surprise field trip will be."

Meg and Greg met Jordan and Anka at the end of the block.

"I bet the surprise will be a trip to Planet Fun," Anka said.

"Or we get to go **swimming**," Greg said.

"But Miss Lin didn't tell us to bring **swimming** stuff," Meg said. "Just bus **passes**."

Jordan broke into a run. "The **faster** we get there, the **faster** Miss Lin will tell us!"

Jordan

Anka

-ing . . .

Miss Lin waited for the class to settle down. "Good **morning**, fifth **graders**! We have an **exciting** day ahead of us."

Jordan whooped. "Are we **going** to the aquarium, Miss Lin?"

Miss Lin smiled. "No, not the aquarium, Jordan. Any other ideas?"

Miss Lin

desk

fist bump

-ing . . .

Miss Lin, Miss Lin! Are we **going** swimming?

No, you will not be **getting** wet. But you will be **taking buses**. And there will be animals.

Are we **going** horseback **riding**?

Dog **sledding**?

No. Not **swimming**, not **riding**, not **sledding**.

When you are all **sitting** quietly, I will be **happy** to tell you!

"We will be **doing** an **Amazing** Quest competition," Miss Lin said. "In teams of two, you will solve clues that send you to three locations around town."

"Like a **scavenger** hunt?" Jordan asked.

Miss Lin nodded. "Yes, exactly. I will give each team a note card with the first of three clues. Solve the clue to find out where to go. When you get there, you will receive a task that you must complete to get the second clue. The **fastest** team to finish all three tasks is the **winner**."

Miss Lin continued. "But if you don't complete a task, you will have to do an *extra* task. And each team will have a parent **tagging** along to help you with the bus travel."

"Get into pairs, and I will hand you the first **Amazing** Quest note cards," Miss Lin said.

"Greg, you and me?" Meg said.

"We can win this thing, Meg!" Greg said, **jumping** up.

"Not if Anka and I are **faster** than you!" Jordan said, **grinning**.

Miss Lin gave a note card to Meg and Greg.

Crack the code **using** the pattern
123 = abc
16-12-1-14-5-20-6-21-14

Cracking the Code

> Crack the code **using**
> the pattern
> 123 = abc
> 16-12-1-14-5-20-6-21-14

Meg sat **staring** at the note card. "One, two, three equals *a*, *b*, *c*. What does that mean?"

Greg was **twirling** his pencil. "It says to use the pattern. So I think one equals *a*, two equals *b* and three equals *c*."

"I get it! And four equals *d* and five equals *e*," Meg said.

Greg nodded. "Let's start by **writing** down the alphabet."

Meg frowned at Greg's pencil. "First we need to **sharpen** this **broken** pencil!"

Let's get **going**!

Using the sharp pencil, Meg made a grid.

It starts with a *P*.

And next is an *L*.

-ing . . .

"Planet Fun is the next stop!" Meg said.

She and Greg hopped off the public bus and ran to the entrance of the theme park.

Greg stepped up to the ticket **counter**. "Hi, we're from Miss Lin's class at Ashton Elementary School."

"You're our first **Amazing** Quest team to arrive!" the man said, **handing** them a note card. "Do you have something to take photos with?"

Greg nodded. "I have my phone."

The man gave them a thumbs-up. "Great. When you finish your task, come back to me for the next clue. Good luck!"

backpack

parent

-ing . . .

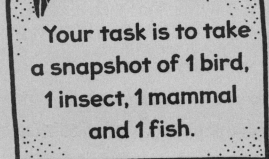

Your task is to take a snapshot of 1 bird, 1 insect, 1 mammal and 1 fish.

"This will be quick!" Meg said. "There are lots of birds **sitting** on those **branches**."

Click!

"Got them. What's next?" Greg said.

"An insect," Meg said, **running** to a **grassy** patch. "There must be an ant **living** in this grass."

"Or a bug **bigger** than an ant!" Greg said, **squinting** at a tall plant. "There is a **grasshopper**!"

Click!

"This task is fun!" Greg said. "What's the next thing **written** on the card?"

Meg looked at the note card. "A mammal."

"No problem!" Greg exclaimed. "I'm a mammal. Take a photo of me!"

Meg laughed as Greg handed her his phone. *Click!*

"What's next?" Greg shouted.

"A fish. That's **harder**," Meg said, **frowning**.

"No it's not!" Greg said, **grinning**. "The Amazon Zone has all sorts of **fishes**."

Inside the Amazon Zone, Meg and Greg ran up the path to the pond.

Amazon Zone plants

Sam the sloth

"There are lots of **fishes swimming** in there!" Meg said, **taking** a shot.

"We are *amazing* at this **Amazing Quest!**" Greg said.

Meg and Greg ran back to the ticket desk.

"That was fast," the man said, **checking** the snapshots and then **handing** them the next note card.

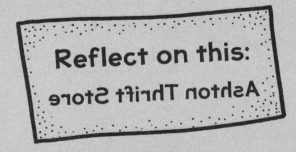

Reflect on this:
Ashton Thrift Store

-ing . . .

Chapter 3

Reflecting on a Hint

"Reflect on this," Meg said, **staring** at the note card. "Why *reflect*?"

The man chuckled. "There's a **handwashing** station at the entrance to the **petting** zoo. It's over there if you—ahem—need it."

Greg frowned. "Um . . . no, thanks. We have to solve this clue and keep **moving**."

"Oh, I know you do. The **handwashing** station may be a good place for *reflecting*," the man said, **winking**.

Meg looked toward the **handwashing** station. She spotted a mirror above the sink, and her eyes got **wider**. "He's **giving** us a hint, Greg! *Reflecting*!"

Meg was **running** across to the sink.

"What, Meg? The next **Amazing** Quest spot is at a sink?"

"No, not exactly. **Reflecting**. We have to *reflect* this," Meg said, **waving** the note card in the air.

sink

"Ashton Thrift Store!" Meg exclaimed, **reading** the image in the mirror. "I love that place. It's in West Plaza."

"That's not far! Let's go," Greg said, already **jogging** to the bus stop.

• • •

At the thrift store, Meg opened the front door, **jingling** a set of bells. She and Greg walked up to the clerk at the sales desk.

"Let me guess," the clerk said, **reaching** into an envelope. "You two are **doing** Miss Lin's **Amazing** Quest!"

"Yes," Meg said. "What's our task?"

"It's on this card," the clerk said, **handing** it to Meg.

After **scanning** the card, Meg said, "We have $10 to get 3 things."

"No problem," Greg said, **marching** up to a rack of shirts and **dresses**.

"The catch is they have to be things for **swimming**," Meg said.

"OK," Greg said. He went across the store to a big bin. "This **swimming** cap is just $1."

hats

vase

$1

odds and ends

mugs and cups

-ing . . .

"Fantastic, Greg!" Meg said, **searching** through the racks of swimwear. "Are these shorts for **swimming**?" She held up a pair of the **longest** shorts she had ever seen.

"Yup, they look like board shorts," Greg said. "How much are they?"

"Five dollars. So that leaves us with four dollars," Meg said. "Let's check in those **boxes**."

Greg picked up a pair of **dusty flippers**. "Here we go!" he said. "And they are exactly four dollars!"

"We are **crushing** this quest!" Meg said.

"Yup! These tasks are fun," Greg said.

swimming cap

flippers

swimming shorts

-ing . . .

Meg and Greg gave the **swimming** cap, shorts and **flippers** to the clerk at the desk.

note card

My first is just **bigger** than nine.
My second is smile less the s.
My third lets the waves rush in.
I am on the map.
Where am I?

-ing . . .

Chapter 4

Solving a Verse

"This is a **tricky** one," Meg said. "What is just **bigger** than nine?"

"That's not hard, Meg," Greg said. "Ten comes after nine."

"Oh, right. Well done," Meg said. "And then a *smile* less the *s*?"

"No big deal," Greg said. "Take away the *s* and you are left with *mile*."

"OK. Ten Mile . . . It must be Ten Mile Inlet!" Meg said, **grinning**.

Greg was **nodding**. "Yes. An inlet *lets* the waves come **rushing** *in*."

Meg started **running** out of the thrift store. "Let's go!"

Meg and Greg ran across the **chilly** sand at Ten Mile Inlet. Miss Lin was **standing** close to several pairs of Meg and Greg's classmates. She had the Ashton mascot, a big red **teddy** bear in her arms.

"Miss Lin! What's the task?" Meg said when they got **closer**.

"This is your third and last task," Miss Lin said, **handing** them a note card.

> Make a bridge for **Teddy** to sit on for 30 seconds. You can use sand, sticks and shells, but no rocks or stones. Make it strong, or **Teddy** will fall!

-ing . . .

Greg looked around the beach at their classmates, all **making** bridges. Jordan and Anka were **putting** the **finishing touches** on theirs.

"Miss Lin," Jordan called. "Can you come and test our bridge now?"

Miss Lin placed **Teddy** in the middle of Jordan and Anka's bridge span. She started **counting**. "One, two, three . . ."

Greg tugged Meg's sleeve. "Come on, Meg. We don't have time to watch! We have to start **collecting** stuff."

"Just wait, Greg. Let's see if their bridge stays up," Meg said.

waves

sand

Teddy

" . . . 12, 13, 14 . . . " Miss Lin said.

Crash! **Teddy** fell.

"Drat!" Anka said, **stomping** the sand.

"Bad luck, kids!" Miss Lin said, **picking** up **Teddy**. "You will have to do the extra task."

. . .

Meg spoke softly to Greg. "We can make a **stronger** bridge than that!"

"Yes, but we have to be quick," Greg said. "Let's go."

skipping ropes

-ing . . .

"They used dry sand for their bridge towers," Meg said, **holding** a load of sticks and shells. "If we make ours with **wetter** sand, the towers will be **stronger**."

"OK, the sand is **wetter** down there," Greg said, **pointing** toward the water.

Meg and Greg ran down the beach and found a flat, **sandy** spot.

"Here is good," Greg said, **kneeling**.

"Let's start with **piling** up the wet sand," Meg said.

Greg nodded. "And we can add shells to make the sand **stronger**."

Meg grinned and picked up a long, wide stick. "And let's use this to make the bridge span."

-ing . . .

Chapter 5

Rushing to Finish

Meg kicked at the sand. "I told you the stick was too **tippy**."

Greg shook his head. "I think it was the sand. It was still too dry."

"Either way, let's be quick. Maybe we can still win this **Amazing** Quest," Meg said. "What's the extra task, Miss Lin?"

Miss Lin pulled out a note card.

Holding it up, Meg read aloud. "Choose one of these tasks: (a) One partner skips rope fifty times, and the other partner pogo hops twenty-five times, or (b) one partner recites the alphabet backward, and the other partner counts down from one hundred by threes."

-ing . . .

skipping

Greg started **swinging** the **skipping** rope.
"1, 2, 3 . . . 15, 16, 17 . . . 34, 35 . . . " The rope fell.
"Darn!"

Meg had started **hopping** on the pogo
stick. She sang with each hop. ". . . 23, 24, 25!
I did it!" she said, **finishing** with an extra hop.

"It turns out, I'm not the **greatest skipper**,"
Greg said, **untangling** the rope for the third
time.

"Try that **flatter** grass, Greg," Meg said.
"I'll count for you."

"And 1, 2, 3 . . . 15, 16 . . . 34. You can do this, Greg!" Meg was **yelling** as Greg got **closer** and **closer**. " . . . 47, 48, 49, 50!"

"You did it!" Meg said.

waves

Miss Lin

skipping rope

-ing . . .

The End

Turn the page for more practice with vowel (and consonant) suffixes!

1-1-1 doubling rule
word sums

For each row, tick the boxes that apply and use that information to decide whether the final consonant of the **base word** needs to be doubled. Then rewrite the word with its suffix attached.

Hint: For more information about the 1-1-1 Doubling Rule, see page 150.

Base word + suffix	1 syllable word	1 short vowel	1 final consonant	Suffix begins with a vowel	Double the final consonant of the base word?	Rewrite word with suffix here
jog + ing	☑	☑	☑	☑	(Yes) / No	jogging
camp + er	☐	☐	☐	☐	Yes / No	
sad + est	☐	☐	☐	☐	Yes / No	
hard + en	☐	☐	☐	☐	Yes / No	
trumpet + ing	☐	☐	☐	☐	Yes / No	
lunch + es	☐	☐	☐	☐	Yes / No	
flat + en	☐	☐	☐	☐	Yes / No	
sad + ly	☐	☐	☐	☐	Yes / No	
sit + ing	☐	☐	☐	☐	Yes / No	
brush + es	☐	☐	☐	☐	Yes / No	
fun + est	☐	☐	☐	☐	Yes / No	
rain + ing	☐	☐	☐	☐	Yes / No	

final e rule
sentence rewrites

Rewrite each sentence's word sum in the space provided.
Hint: For more information about the Final e Rule, see page 151.

1. My dog is **brave + er** than your dog.
   My dog is _____ than your dog.

2. I went to get five **lime + s** at the store.
   I went to get five _____ at the store.

3. I like **cheese + y** snacks.
   I like _____ snacks.

4. **Hope + ful + ly** it will be sunny.
   _____ it will be sunny.

5. This wagon is **use + ful**.
   This wagon is _____ .

6. That cat is the **cute + est**!
   That cat is the _____ !

7. My sister was **snore + ing** in the car.
   My sister was _____ in the car.

8. I am not **blame + ing** you.
   I am not _____ you.

9. Tim rode his bike **safe + ly** along the path.
   Tim rode his bike _____ along the path.

10. Meg gave Greg a **broke + en** stick.
    Meg gave Greg a _____ stick.

-ing . . .

All the stories in this book introduce words that have a **suffix** or a **prefix**.

This story focuses on words that use the suffix *-ed*. This **suffix** can be pronounced in three different ways: /id/, /t/ and /d/. For example, listen to the sounds made by the *-ed* suffixes in this sentence: *I was so **excited**, I **jumped** up and **hugged** my mom.*

To build their vocabulary, it's helpful for children to know the meaning of the suffix *-ed:*

-ed indicates an action that happened in the past (*barked*) or means "a characteristic of" (*a four-legged animal*).

Note: Adding *-ed* to put an action into the past (a past-tense verb) is very common, but there are also many action words that don't follow this pattern. They are called irregular past-tense verbs (*run → ran, sleep → slept, swim → swam*). This is a good opportunity to discuss irregular verbs with your child.

For a list of *-ed* suffix words, including all the ones used in this story, and a list of common irregular past-tense verbs, go to megandgregbooks.com.

This story introduces a third rule for adding suffixes: the Final *y* Rule (*tried, carried, laziness, joyful, played*). The story also uses the two suffix rules introduced in the previous story: the 1-1-1 Doubling Rule and the Final *e* Rule. See pages 150–152 for information on how these rules work.

Grated, Chopped, Crushed

A story featuring the suffix

-ed

maze

wagged

Chapter 1

Planned

Greg ran to catch up with Meg and Anka as they **walked** outside for recess. "Do either of you want to do the science fair project with me?" he **asked**.

Anka shook her head. "I'm doing one with Jordan. We plan to test how sunflower plants grow in different soils. Miss Lin already **approved** it."

Meg **smiled**. "I'll do the science fair project with you, Greg."

"Great!" Greg said and then **looked** sideways at Meg. "But could we do something other than, um, plants?"

Meg **tried** not to laugh. "Sure. Got any ideas?"

"Yes! Let's test Rocket riding on the back of my bike," Greg said.

"Poor Rocket!" Meg said. "What if he falls off and gets hurt?"

Anka **nodded**. "Ask Miss Lin if you can use the class hamsters."

Greg **clapped** his hands. "That's it! Buster and Chomper can ride on the back of my bike!"

"No!" Meg said. "What if *they* fall off and get hurt?"

hamsters   bike

Greg **sighed**. "OK, fine. I guess that's not my best idea."

Meg thought for a second. "How about if we build a maze for the hamsters?"

"That sounds fun!" Anka said. "Maybe you could time how fast they run through it?"

"Yes, OK." Greg **scratched** his chin. "A hamster maze!"

After recess Meg and Greg **asked** Miss Lin if they could borrow the class hamsters for their science fair project.

hamster hutch

Miss Lin **smiled**. "Tell me more."

"We plan to make a maze for the hamsters," Greg said.

"And not just for fun. We will get the hamsters to run in the maze," Meg **added**.

"OK, and what will you test with hamsters running in the maze?" Miss Lin **asked**.

Greg **jumped** up and swung his arms like a runner.

Meg **grinned**. "We will test which hamster runs fastest."

Miss Lin **nodded**. "OK, that's a good start. Think about how you will get the hamsters to run from the beginning to the end of your maze. Will you give them a reason to run?"

Meg and Greg **looked** at each other and then back at Miss Lin.

"Could we put different kinds of hamster treats at the end of the maze for them?" Greg **asked**.

Meg **clapped**. "Yes! That's a great idea, Greg. We can find out how fast they get through the maze to eat each yummy snack."

"You're well on your way to designing a good experiment," Miss Lin **replied**.

-ed

"So can we do this experiment with the class hamsters?" Meg **asked**.

Miss Lin **smiled**. "I think that will be fine. Which of you will have them?"

"I will," Greg said.

"OK. Check with your mom and dad. If they say yes, then you can take them home," Miss Lin said.

Greg **grinned**. "OK!"

"Thank you, Miss Lin!" Meg said.

-ed

Chapter 2

Constructed

potted plant

After dinner that evening, Meg **called** Greg. "Did your mom and dad say you could bring the hamsters home?"

"Yup! As long as I look after them," Greg said. "You'll help me with that, right?"

Meg **laughed**. "Of course, Greg! Do you want to come over here to start planning our maze?"

"Great!" Greg **replied**. "I'm on my way. I'm bringing Rocket with me."

-ed

At Meg's house, she, Greg and Rocket sat on her bedroom floor.

Meg **grabbed** a notepad. "Let's make a list of all the things that go in a maze."

Greg **scratched** his chin. "OK. Tunnels, ramps, arches."

"And lots of twists and turns," Meg said.

Greg **nodded**. "Yes, but it can't be so hard that the hamsters get lost."

"That's why we use hamster snacks to tempt them," said Meg.

lamp

shelf

basket

Rocket

"What will we use to build the maze?" Greg **asked**.

"Cardboard," Meg **replied**. She **jumped** up. "Let's see what we can find in the recycling bin."

Greg **followed** Meg into the kitchen and **studied** the contents of the bin. He **reached** in and **grabbed** a plastic yogurt tub. "We can make this into a wheel for the hamsters! Here, Rocket, hold this for me, please."

plastic tub

"Great," Meg said, "and look at all this cardboard we can use for the walls."

"And these toilet rolls are perfect little tubes for tunnels," Greg said.

-ed

Meg **sketched** the lines for the maze walls on a flat base.

Rocket

Greg cut strips of card to make the walls.

They stuck all the walls on the base.

Meg **grabbed** six tubes to make tunnels.

tubes

cards

Greg **poked** a hole in the plastic tub and **fitted** a pen in it.

The next day Greg took his old red wagon to school, and after school he and Meg **pulled** the hamster hutch to his house. Meg and Greg **lifted** the hutch off the wagon and **carried** it inside. Rocket **sniffed** the hutch and **wagged** his tail.

"My mom said we can keep the hamsters in the den," Greg said.

Meg **nodded**. "OK, I'll run back home and bring over the maze."

A few minutes later, Meg set the maze on the floor of Greg's den.

Greg **unlatched** the door of the hutch and **picked** up Chomper. "Time to test the maze!"

hutch

Chomper

Buster

door

-ed

maze

Greg **nudged** Chomper into the start of the maze. The hamster **sniffed** at the walls for a bit and then **scampered** off along the path.

Meg **clapped**. "It's a hit!"

"Buster, your turn next," Greg said.

Buster went along the first path in the maze, but . . .

"Yikes!" Greg said. "Buster is stuck."

Meg bit her lip. "It's the arches. We cut them too small."

Greg **nodded**. "And Buster is a lot bigger than Chomper."

-ed

Chapter 3

Tested

Meg and Greg **started** fixing their maze.
Greg cut the arches wider. Meg **removed**
the toilet-roll tunnels.

"Let's see if Buster will fit now," Meg said.

Greg **picked** up Buster and **placed** him
right in front of one of the arches. "Try
walking through, Buster." Greg gently
nudged him.

"Good job, Buster!" Meg said as the
hamster **waddled** through the arch and
slowly along a path in the maze.

Greg **frowned**. "Buster seems pretty
sleepy. Let's start the experiment with
Chomper."

"OK, Greg," Meg said. "But first let's get the hamster snacks for the end of the maze."

Greg **nodded**. "Yup. What do hamsters like?"

"Let's check online," Meg said.

Greg **jumped** up. "We have carrots in the fridge." He **dashed** to the kitchen.

"Cut them up into small chunks," Meg **called** after him.

shelf

carpet

maze

Greg came back with a bowl full of carrots. "I **grated** them."

"Perfect," Meg said.

Rocket **looked** up from his dog bed and **sniffed** the air.

"Not for you, Rocket!" Greg said.

Meg **smiled**. "We can time both hamsters with the carrots today, and then tomorrow we can try something different."

"Good idea," Greg said as he **placed** a small pile of **grated** carrot at the end of the maze.

Meg **carried** Chomper to the maze and held him at the starting line.

Greg **perched** on a chair with a timer in his hand. "Let him go on 1 . . . 2 . . . 3!"

Chomper **rushed** along the paths and under the arches.

Meg **clapped** softly. "I think he can smell the carrots!"

"Go, Chomper, go!" Greg said.

Chomper **darted** across the finish line.

"56 seconds!" Greg **yelled**.

Rocket **jumped** up and **barked**.

-ed

Greg **laughed**. "Don't scare the hamsters, Rocket!"

Rocket **whined** and **tugged** on Greg's pant leg.

"Not now, Rocket," Greg said. "I have to write down Chomper's time."

Meg **scooped** up the hamster and **petted** his head. "You did so well, Chomper!" She **carried** him back to the hutch. "Your turn, Buster. Buster? Greg, where's Buster?"

Greg **turned** to Meg. "In the hutch. Isn't he?"

"Nope, and the door is **unlatched**," Meg said. "I think he has **escaped**."

Greg got up. "Is he hiding in a corner?"

"No, Greg. Buster is not in here," Meg said.

Rocket **barked** softly.

Ruff, ruff!

hutch

door

Chapter 4

Escaped!

Meg and Greg stood next to the hamster hutch and **stared** at it.

"This is bad!" Greg said. "I **promised** to look after the hamsters."

"Don't worry, Greg. Buster can't have gone far." Meg knelt down, put Chomper into the hutch and **latched** the door.

Rocket **barked** again.

"Quiet, Rocket. We need to find Buster," Greg said.

"Let's start by checking under the armchair," Meg said.

Greg carefully **tilted** the armchair and Meg **checked** under it. "Nope."

Rocket **tugged** on Greg's socks.

Greg **turned** to Rocket. "OK, that's it. You have to go." Greg led his dog into the hall. "Sit there," he said, shutting the door.

Back in the den, Meg **lifted** a corner of the carpet.

"Under the carpet?" Greg **asked**.

"I'm checking for holes," Meg said.

"Holes?" Greg **gasped**.

Meg **looked** at Greg. "Yes, holes. Hamsters are so tiny they can fit into little holes or cracks."

Greg **frowned**. "But Buster isn't *that* tiny. He couldn't fit through the arches in our first maze!"

Meg **shrugged**. "He's still small."

Greg **clutched** his hair in his fists. "You mean Buster could have **escaped** from the den?"

Meg **nodded**. "Sure, he could have. My friend's hamster once **ended** up under the floorboards."

Greg **stared** at Meg. "Are you serious? How will we ever find Buster?"

-ed

"We have to think like a hamster," Meg said.

"OK, I can do that," Greg said. He **dropped** to the floor and crept along, checking the walls for cracks and holes. He **stopped** suddenly. "Meg, this air vent. It has hamster-**sized** gaps!"

Meg bit her lip.

"Do you think Buster went in there?" Greg **asked**.

"I hope not!" Meg said.

air vent

carpet

99
-ed

Meg **crouched** and **looked** into the vent. "Where does this lead to?"

Greg **shrugged**. "I don't know, but our kitchen is on the other side of this wall. Let's check if the vent goes through to there."

Greg **opened** the den door, and he and Meg **headed** into the kitchen. While they were searching for a vent opening, they could hear Rocket barking.

"Is Rocket back in the den?" Meg **asked**.

Greg **frowned**. "You're right. It sounds like it. And that's not his normal bark."

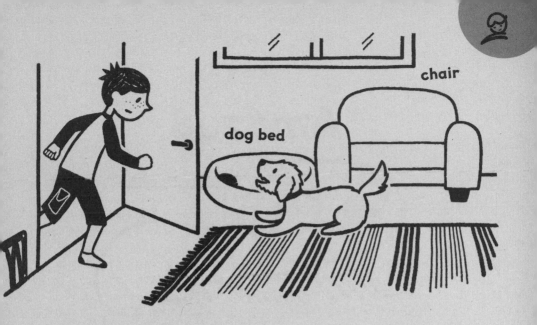

dog bed

chair

Greg **jogged** back to the den. "What's up, Rocket?"

Rocket was sitting next to his dog bed. He **barked** softly.

"Why are you barking like that?" Greg **asked** as he went to fetch Rocket. Suddenly he **gasped**. "Meg!"

Meg came in. "Is it Buster?"

Greg **grinned**. "Not just Buster!"

Chapter 5

Amazed

Meg and Greg **stared** down at the dog bed. Buster was **curled** up with five little hamster babies.

"I guess Buster isn't a boy hamster!" Meg said.

Greg shook his head. "This explains why Buster wasn't **interested** in our maze."

Meg **nodded**. "And why he—I mean *she*—was too big to fit through the arches!"

Greg knelt down and put his arm around Rocket. "You knew, didn't you, buddy?"

Rocket **barked** again.

Meg **smiled**. "They are so small!"

Greg **nodded**. "And hairless. Not exactly cute."

"They will be when they get bigger," Meg said. "But what do we do with Buster and five hamster pups?"

"I think we had better tell Miss Lin," Greg said. "But first let's tell my mom."

-ed

Greg's mom **laughed** when she heard the news. "Well, that's a surprise! Why don't you call Jenkin's Pet Shop for some advice?"

"Good idea," Meg said.

By suppertime, Buster and her pups were **settled** in their own hutch, on loan from the pet shop. Rocket slept **curled** up next to them on the den floor.

"I guess this changes our science fair project," Greg said.

Meg **nodded**. "On Monday we can ask Miss Lin for more time to do our experiment."

When Meg and Greg spoke with Miss Lin, she **yelped** in surprise.

"Buster had pups?" she said. "The pet shop said Buster was a male hamster and so was Chomper."

Greg **scratched** his chin. "I think Chomper still is male."

Miss Lin **smiled**. "Yes, I think so as well!"

"So can we have extra time to do the project?" Meg **asked**.

Miss Lin **agreed** that Meg and Greg could have an extra month for their science fair project.

"That will give the little pups time to grow," Miss Lin said.

• • •

Every day after school, Meg went over to Greg's house to help care for the hamsters. One day she was putting freshly **grated** carrot in the hutch for them and an idea **flashed** into her mind.

"Greg, I have a great idea," Meg **announced**. "Now that the pups are four weeks old, let's do our experiment with all the hamsters, not just Chomper and Buster."

hamster pups

-ed

Greg **nodded**. "That's a perfect plan! We can test if the pups and adults like the same or different snacks."

"Yes, and we can compare the time it takes for pups and adults to finish the maze," Meg said. "I bet the pups will get to the snacks faster."

Greg **shrugged**. "We will have to test them."

Meg **smiled**. "Well, we have a lot to do. Let's get **started**!"

grated carrots

Hamster Running Times in Seconds
by Meg and Greg

	Grated carrots	Chopped grapes	Crushed nuts
Chomper	56	42	55
Buster	64	60	62
Pup 1	59	48	57
Pup 2	57	43	57
Pup 3	60	50	60
Pup 4	63	52	
Pup 5	63	51	

The End

Turn the page for more practice with -ed (and other suffixes)!

suffix -ed
word rewrites

Hint: Remember to consider the 1-1-1 Doubling Rule and the Final e Rule. For more information, see pages 150–151.

Rewrite the action word (verb) in these sentences by adding the suffix *-ed* to put the action in the past (past tense).

1. They **jog** on the path. _____

2. I **bake** a cake. _____

3. We **jump** off the rock. _____

4. The cat **stretches**. _____

5. The dog **barks**. _____

Rewrite the action word (verb) in these sentences by removing the suffix *-ed* to put the action in the present (present tense).

1. I **trimmed** my hair. _____

2. They **smiled** at the winner. _____

3. I **biked** with my dad. _____

4. We **grabbed** a snack. _____

5. The cat **hunted** a bird. _____

final y rule
word sums

Hint: Remember to consider the Final y Rule.
For more information, see page 152.

Base word + suffix	Rewrite word with suffix here
copy + er	
copy + ing	
empty + ed	
fairy + es	
dizzy + ing	
family + es	
marry + ed	
silly + est	
study + ed	
study + ing	
candy + ed	

Also available at megandgregbooks.com

All the stories in this
book introduce words that
have a **suffix** or a **prefix**.
This story focuses on words with prefixes.
The prefixes introduced in this story differ from
the suffixes in the previous stories in that we
don't need to adjust the **base word**. We simply
add the prefix to the front of the base word.
The prefixes we include are *de-*, *dis-*,
ex-, *in-*, *pre-*, *re-* and *un-*. There are other
common prefixes, such as *non-* and *sub-*,
that we haven't included.

To build their vocabulary, it's helpful for children
to know the meanings of the prefixes in this story:

de- means "opposite of" (*decompose*) or "down/
away" (*deflate*).

dis- means "opposite of" (*disconnect*).

ex- means "out of" (*exhale*).

in- means "in or into" (*inhale*) or "not" (*insane*).

pre- means "before" (*precook*).

re- means "back" (*return*) or "again" (*rerun*).

un- means "not" (*unhappy*) or "opposite of"
(*unzip*).

For a list of prefix words, including all
the ones used in this story, go to
megandgregbooks.com.

Extreme Pumpkin Patching

A story featuring prefixes

Meg the cat

de-, dis-, ex-, in-, pre-, re-, un-

corn

extremely big pumpkin

Chapter 1

Get **Prepared**

"My super hero costume is super **uncomfortable**," Greg complained. He and Meg were walking to school.

"I **refuse** to wear anything **uncomfy**! This cat onesie is soft and cozy," Meg **replied**.

Greg laughed. "And it's all white! **Remember** we're going to the pumpkin patch today."

Meg shrugged. "So?"

"You'll get it covered in mud!" Greg said.

Meg grinned. "**Relax**, Greg. I've got boots. And besides, it's going to be an easy day. All we're doing is keeping an eye on our little kindergarten buddies."

Greg smiled. "Yup, it will be fun! The best part will be the corn maze. The farm has **expanded** it."

"Corn mazes can be scary," Meg said. "I **prefer** picking the pumpkins. And going on wagon rides!"

Greg nodded. "The farm has those as well. I have a map."

carved pumpkins

ex- . . .

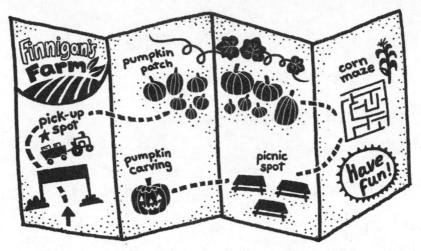

At school Miss Lin clapped her hands. "Good morning, fifth graders! Today is our Halloween field trip to the pumpkin patch at Finnigan's Farm. Your kindergarten buddies are very **excited**!"

Greg raised his hand. "Can we get *two* pumpkins, Miss Lin?"

Miss Lin smiled. "Sure. Just be **prepared** to carry them both and help your kindergarten buddy at the same time. **Remember** to let your buddy **decide** which activities they want to do on the farm."

"Miss Lin?" Greg asked. "Can we go into the corn maze?"

"Yes," Miss Lin said, "as long as you are back on the bus in time for the **return** trip."

"Can we take **unlimited** wagon rides?" Meg asked.

"Yes, but it all **depends** on your buddy. Ask them what they **prefer**," Miss Lin said.

Meg grinned. "This will be so fun!"

Meg the cat

mask

cape

ex- . . .

Meg and Greg's class met the kindergarteners by the bus. Miss Lin and the kindergarten teacher had a list and were pairing students with their buddies.

"Meg and Greg, you will be with Rose and Libby," Miss Lin said, beckoning to two little girls dressed in identical fairy costumes. She stuck name labels on them. "Do you **remember** the twins, Rose and Libby, from our last field trip?"

"Actually, Miss Lin . . ." The kindergarten teacher smiled as she **removed** the name labels and **reapplied** each on the opposite child. "*This* is Rose, and *this* is Libby."

Libby
Rose

Libby
Rose

Meg smiled at Rose. "I like your fairy costume!"

Rose smiled in **return** and slipped her hand into Meg's. "You are a cat."

"Yes," Meg said. "I am Meg the cat."

Greg bent to Libby's level. "Hi Libby, I'm Greg."

"I have fairy wings," Libby said, **unzipping** her jacket.

"Those are cute, Libby," Greg said. "Let's get on the bus."

Rose

Libby

cape

mask

ex- . . .

Libby got halfway up the bus steps and turned around. "Fairies can fly!" she whispered.

Greg nodded and followed her onto the bus.

"I am **excellent** at flying!" Libby said as she clambered up the back of a bus seat and launched herself into the air.

"Libby! That's **extremely unsafe!**" Greg caught her in midair and put her back on her feet. "Let's go and sit down."

Herb, the bus driver, chuckled. "Well done, Greg. You sure have your hands full today. You should have **predicted** that a fairy would try to fly!" Herb winked at Greg.

ex-...

Greg **exhaled** and led Libby to an empty spot.

OK, kids! **Remember**, no standing up as I drive.

That **includes** you, Libby.

Libby

I am not Libby. I am a fairy!

~~Libby~~ fairy

OK, that **includes** you, fairy.

ex- . . .

Chapter 2

Sit Back and **Relax**

Herb closed the doors, and the bus rumbled down the street toward Finnigan's Farm.

Meg looked out the window. From behind she felt a little hand on her head.

"Let's see if cats can fly too." Libby giggled as she **removed** Meg's cat ears and flung them across the bus.

"**Excuse** me, Libby. Those are my ears," Meg said, reaching to take them from a classmate.

Rose **exploded** in a fit of giggles and tried to rub off Meg's cat nose.

"Rose, Libby!" Greg said. "Let's **decide** which activity to do first when we get to the farm."

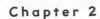

"Pumpkin patch!" Rose said.

"Corn maze!" Libby said.

Greg nodded. "We can go to the pumpkin patch first and the corn maze after."

"Yes. Pumpkin patch first!" Rose **declared**.

"No. Corn maze first!" Libby **demanded**.

Meg turned to Greg. "Yikes!"

Meg the cat

Herb pulled into Finnigan's Farm.

"We're here!" Greg said. He pointed out the window. "Girls, look at that huge **inflatable** pumpkin!"

"Can we take it home?" Rose asked.

"No, but we can take real pumpkins home," Meg said.

Libby squealed. "Let's go!"

Herb opened the bus doors. "Careful as you **disembark**, kids. Have fun! The bus **returns** at two o'clock."

A hay wagon stood ready to take the kids for a ride to the pumpkin patch.

Rose and Libby called out at the same time. "Wagon ride!"

Greg **exhaled**. "Phew. They agree on something!"

Meg and Greg helped Rose and Libby up the steps onto the wagon.

"Let's sit on this bale," Meg said.

"I sit here," Rose **declared**.

Libby jumped up next to Rose. For a second they sat still.

The driver spoke to the wagon full of kids. "Sit back and **relax**. Next stop is the pumpkin patch. Let's sing a song!"

wagon ride

The wagon driver started to sing. "Old MacDonald had a farm, E-I-E-I-O!"

Everybody joined in as the wagon trundled along a muddy track. "And on that farm, he had a—"

"Fairy!" Rose shouted.

The driver laughed. "This is an **unusual** farm!" The song continued. "And on that farm, he had a fairy—"

Slam! The tractor's back wheel rolled into a deep mud puddle.

Slop! Mud flew into the wagon. *Splatter!*

wagon

mud

126

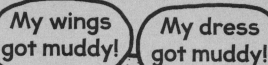

My wings got muddy!

My dress got muddy!

Meg the cat

Ack! I got mud on me as well.

I did not **expect** all this mud.

Like I **predicted**, Meg.

Meg **unzipped** her backpack and checked her lunch box for a napkin.

The driver pressed hard on the gas to get the wagon **unstuck**.

Lurch!

The wagon bumped along the muddy track.

Chapter 3

An **Extremely** Big Pumpkin

The wagon slid to a stop in the pumpkin patch.

"I feel sick," Rose whispered. "My tummy hurts."

"Me too. That was a bumpy ride," Meg said.

As they got off the wagon, Miss Lin handed out **reusable** bags to carry the pumpkins. Rose opened her bag and promptly threw up into it. She handed the bag to Meg.

"Ugh," Meg gasped.

"Oh dear," Miss Lin said, taking the bag from Meg and giving her another. "Meg, why don't you take Rose to sit down and rest for a bit?"

Rose slumped in the mud next to a big pumpkin.

pumpkin

That was **unlucky**. The bumpy ride made you **unwell**.

Rose

Can this be my pumpkin?

Um, it's **extremely** big . . .

That's OK.

Rose jumped up and started running to her sister. Libby was at the far edge of the pumpkin patch.

pumpkin patch

"I guess you're feeling better," Meg said to herself as she got up and followed Rose. In the **distance** she could see Greg **desperately** trying to stop Libby from jumping on top of the pumpkins.

"I found a big, BIG pumpkin!" Rose yelled.

Libby glanced at Rose and then started looking for her own big pumpkin.

"I'm glad Rose **distracted** Libby," Greg said when Meg joined him. "She was **destroying** perfectly good pumpkins."

Meg twirled her hair. "Like Herb said, these kids are a handful!"

Greg nodded. "Yup!"

Suddenly Rose yelled, "*My* pumpkin!"

"No! *My* pumpkin! You bad fairy!" Libby stomped in the mud.

Rose burst into **unhappy** sobs.

Meg **exhaled**.

"Libby! No **insults**!" Greg called. "There are lots of pumpkins."

Rose

pumpkins

Libby

Rose clung to Meg and sobbed into her
white cat costume, adding snot to the mud.

"Ugh," Meg said, **exhaling**. She gently
detached Rose's muddy fists from her
costume. "Let's go over that way and look
for a nice little pumpkin."

Rose sniffed and nodded. "But it has to be
a big pumpkin. Bigger than Libby's."

"Well, let's see what we find," Meg said.
"It has to fit into our **reusable** bag."

"This pumpkin!" Rose said. "I ♥ this big pumpkin!"

Meg bent to **inspect** it. "Let's give it the bag test."

Rip!

"That's **unlucky**, Rose. Let's pick a smaller pumpkin," Meg said.

Rose stomped on the **decomposing** vines. "No! This **exact** pumpkin!"

Meg **inhaled**. She picked up the pumpkin and staggered to the pumpkin-carving tent.

pumpkin patch

Pumpkin carving

Chapter 4

Disgusting
Pumpkin Gunk

"This pumpkin is **unbelievably** heavy! My arms are about to **detach** from my body," Meg groaned. She **deposited** the pumpkin on a table with a thud.

"It will be lighter once we **remove** all the seeds and stringy bits of pulp," Greg said.

Meg beckoned to the girls. "Come on, Libby and Rose. It's pumpkin-carving time."

"This will be fun!" Greg said.

Meg blew the hair out of her eyes. "You're so positive, Greg."

"Well, pumpkin carving *is* fun," Greg said. "And anyways, what could go wrong?"

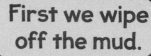

Let's prepare to carve the pumpkins.

First we wipe off the mud.

cloth

Then we take off the tops and get rid of all the stringy gunk.

Libby

Rose and Libby stared at Meg and Greg.

And you are going to help us.

That's a bit unlikely, Greg.

Greg cut around the stem of each pumpkin and yanked off the tops. "Now we scoop out all the gunk and save the seeds to eat later."

"I like pumpkin seeds!" Libby said. "Can I eat them now?"

"Not yet. They're **uncooked** and covered in slime!" Greg said.

Libby looked **disappointed**.

"You can take some home and cook them," Meg said.

Rose **inspected** the pumpkin. "That looks gross." She sniffed. "And it smells **disgusting**! I'm not eating any!"

Rose

pumpkin gunk

ex- . . .

pumpkin
top

Libby picked up a handful of the
pumpkin gunk and flung it at Rose.
"Duck!" she yelled.

Rose grinned, grabbed the gunk off
her dress and **deposited** it onto Greg's
cape.

"Libby, Rose! This is **extremely
unhelpful!**" Greg said.

Meg flung her hands in the air. "OK,
I think it's time to go and **explore** the
corn maze!"

Chapter 5

Exploring
the Corn Maze

Meg and Greg led Libby and Rose to the corn maze.

"Pumpkin slime is dripping down my neck," Greg said.

Meg smiled. "You sound **unimpressed**."

"That's because I *am* **unimpressed**!" Greg groaned.

Miss Lin trotted over. "On your way to the corn maze? You can leave your pumpkins here. You have fifteen minutes left before the bus **returns**."

"I can't wait," Greg muttered.

Libby and Rose skipped into the corn maze. "What do we do in here?" Libby asked.

"It's a maze," Greg said. "We go along the paths and hunt for the **exit**."

Libby crossed her arms. "That's boring. I am **unimpressed**." She grinned. "Like you, Greg! *Unimpressed*."

Swish! Swish!

Rose grabbed Meg's hand. "What's that?"

"I'm scared," Rose whispered.

Meg squeezed Rose's hand. "It's just a fan from one of those big **inflatable** things, like the big pumpkin we saw when we arrived at the farm. Let's go and find out what it is."

Meg and Rose tiptoed around the corner toward the swishing noise.

"A cat! A cat just like you, Meg!" Rose and Libby ran and hugged the **inflatable** cat.

Whoosh! The cat **deflated**.

"Careful," Greg said. "Let's look for more **inflatable** things."

corn

deflated cat

"More cats?" Libby asked.

"Cats, witches, pumpkins. Those sorts of things," Meg said.

Libby and Rose held hands and skipped along, splashing in the mud. "We are hunting for cats and witches and pumpkins!" they sang.

Swish! Swish! Ha. Ha. Ha!

Libby and Rose stopped skipping. "What was that?" Libby **demanded**.

They all crept to the corner and . . .

ex- . . .

A huge skeleton loomed over the path. Rose and Libby screamed and began to run, slipping and sliding through the mud.

Greg looked at Meg. "It seems the skeleton is a little **unpopular!**"

Meg shrugged. "Well, it was **unexpected!** It scared them."

Meg and Greg ran after the girls. "Libby, Rose! Stay with us!"

Where are you?

corn maze

Rose

In here! Stuck in the mud!

Yikes! Let's get you **unstuck**, Libby.

Carry me!

And me!

OK, let's go.

It's time to **return** to the bus! We are **departing** shortly.

The End

Turn the page for more practice with prefixes!

prefixes
crossword

Hint: Remember that prefixes have meanings.
For more information, see page 112.

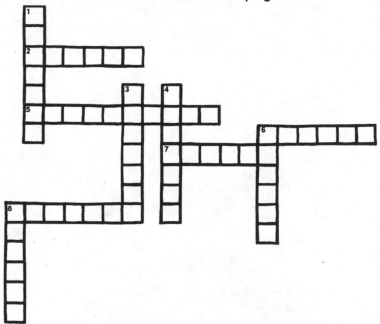

Across →

2. To **breathe out** is to __hale.
5. The **opposite** of **connect**.
6. To **pack** your bag **again**.
7. To **breathe in** is to __hale.
8. The **opposite** of **lucky**.

Down ↓

1. If you **made** your lunch the night **before** going to school, you ___ your lunch.
3. **Not happy**.
4. To **visit** something **again**.
6. To take a library book **back** is to __**turn** it.
8. The **opposite** of **safe**.

prefixes
word search

Find the words listed below in the puzzle.
Words are hidden ➜ and ↓

p j i n f e c t r z s z
r d e l e t e r e p e z
e d r i t k w e f r z k
b e e p u l e s i e i u
a f f b n b x e l p h n
k l u c w j i l l l s p
e a n d i d t l n a o l
f t d i s c a r d n f u
d e c t e u n s a f e g
e x p l o d e j l p n k
e x b m r e i n j e c t

deflate	infect	refund
delete	inject	resell
discard	prebake	unplug
exit	preplan	unsafe
explode	refill	unwise

Also available at megandgregbooks.com

ex- . . .

Some oddities of English explained

Do you know what's tricky about these words?

by, my

In these words, the vowel makes a long ī sound. *Meg and Greg* Book 6 will cover long vowels.

here

This word is pronounced /hee-er/, which is a bit unexpected. Some people consider this word and others like it (*fire, sphere*) to be a mixture of a **magic *e*** word and an ***r*-controlled vowel** word.

said

This common word is pronounced /sed/. It is the past tense of *say*, but the pronunciation of the vowel team *ai* is unexpected. The expected way would be a long ā sound, as in *pay → paid.*

they

This word uses the uncommon vowel team *ey*, which in this case is pronounced with a long ā sound. In other cases, *ey* is pronounced with a long ē sound (*key*).

your

This word has the three-letter *r*-controlled vowel *our* making the sound /or/. There are only a few words that use *our* in this way (*four, pour*).

Tricky words introduced in Books 1–4

a	do, to	of	when
"all" family (ball, small, etc.)	go, no, so	OK	where
as, has	have, give	the	which
	I	was	why
be, he, me, we, she	is, his	what	you

Please refer to megandgregbooks.com for explanations of these tricky words.

A note about word meanings and etymology

It's fun to pull words apart and understand how they were built. For example, the word *unzip* can be pulled apart: *un-* is the **prefix** meaning "opposite of," and *zip* is the **base word** meaning "the action of doing up a zipper." So *unzip* means "the action of undoing a zipper."

But not all prefix and **suffix** meanings are obvious when you try to pull a word apart. What about the word *exhale*? By taking off the prefix *ex-* we are left with *hale*. This isn't a stand-alone word in English, so we don't know what it means until we dig into its history. It turns out that *hale* is a **root** that comes from the Latin word *halare*, meaning "to breathe." Once we know this, it's easier to pull apart *exhale*: *ex-* is the prefix meaning "out of" and *hale* relates to breathing, so *exhale* means "the action of breathing out."

If you are confused by a word and want to learn more about its history or why it might be spelled the way it is, try looking in an **etymology** dictionary.

What is the 1-1-1 Doubling Rule?

The 1-1-1 Doubling Rule helps a child figure out when to double the final **consonant** of the **base word** before they add a suffix to that word.

Here is the rule: If the base word has 1 syllable, 1 short vowel and 1 final consonant *and* the suffix starts with a vowel, then you double the final consonant of the base word before adding the suffix. So you examine the base word and the suffix and need to say yes to four things to use the 1-1-1 Doubling Rule.

Examples of when to double: *sit + ing = sitting, drop + ed = dropped, sad + er = sadder, sun + y = sunny.*

Examples of when not to double: *gallop + ing = galloping, rain + ing = raining, camp + ed = camped, sad + ly = sadly.*

To get children started with the 1-1-1 Doubling Rule, try using a table like the one below.

Base word + suffix	1 syllable word	1 short vowel	1 final consonant	Suffix begins with a vowel	Double the final consonant of the base word?	Rewrite word with suffix here
run + ing	☑	☑	☑	☑	Yes / No	running
hard + en	☑	☐	☐	☑	Yes / No	harden
fast + er	☐	☐	☐	☐	Yes / No	
big + est	☐	☐	☐	☐	Yes / No	
help + ful	☐	☐	☐	☐	Yes / No	
garden + ing	☐	☐	☐	☐	Yes / No	

When children are more comfortable with the rule, they can draw four small circles on their page when they come across a word that needs a suffix added to it. They can then think about the word and suffix, and tick the circles that answer yes to each question: Does it have 1 syllable? Does it have 1 short vowel? And so on. This will help them do a quick check to be sure they use the rule correctly.

What is the Final *e* Rule?

The Final *e* Rule helps a child figure out when to drop the silent final *e* of the **base word** before they add a suffix to that word.

Here is the rule: If the base word ends in a final silent *e*, then look at the first letter of the suffix being added. If the suffix begins with a vowel, then drop the final silent *e* from the base word. If the suffix begins with a consonant, then keep the final silent *e* on the base word.

Examples of when to drop the final silent *e*:
brave + est = bravest, hope + ed = hoped, horse + ing = horsing.

Examples of when to keep the final silent *e*: *brave + ly = bravely, hope + ful = hopeful, horse + less = horseless.*

Note: For a word like *baker* (*bake + -er*), children often ask if they really need to drop the final silent *e* and add **-er**. Can't they just add the letter *r*? It's worth explaining that the letter *r* has no meaning by itself. The suffix **-er** does. It's important for children to understand that they aren't just adding the letter *r*. They are removing the final silent *e* and adding the suffix **-er**.

bik¢ + ing = biking

safe + ly = safely

What is the Final y Rule?

The Final y Rule helps a child figure out when to change the final y of the **base word** to *i* before they add a suffix to that word.

Here is the rule: If the base word ends in the letter y, then change the y to i and add the suffix (it doesn't matter if it's a vowel suffix or a consonant suffix). However, there are some notable exceptions: (1) If the suffix itself starts with the letter *i*, then leave the y alone and just add the suffix (this avoids a double *i*). (2) If the base word ends in a vowel + y (*oy, ay, ey*), then leave the y on the base word and just add the suffix.

Examples of changing the y to i: *copy + er = copier, silly + est = silliest, lazy + ness = laziness.*

Examples of leaving the y alone: *copy + ing = copying, joy + ful = joyful.*

Note: When you add the suffix **-s** to a base word ending in a y, you actually need to add **-es** (*fly* ➔ *flies*, *lady* ➔ *ladies*).

$$fairy^i + es = fairies$$

$$play + ing = playing$$

About the
Meg and Greg stories

Who are the *Meg and Greg* stories for?

These **decodable** stories are for all children who are learning how to read, and they are especially helpful for children who have **dyslexia** or another language-based learning difficulty. All children benefit from learning English incrementally, so the *Meg and Greg* stories introduce one concept at a time, with each story building on the previous ones.

We wrote the stories for learning readers who are ages 6 to 9 (approximately grades 2–4), which is a little older than when many kids start learning to read. These slightly older learners can understand and appreciate more complex content, but they often need it written at a lower reading level. You might see this concept described with the term *hi-lo*.

To make a hi-lo concept work for children who are emerging readers, we designed the *Meg and Greg* stories for shared reading. A buddy reader—an adult or other confident reader—shares the reading with the child who is learning. Each story has five short chapters and is ideal for use in one-on-one or small-group reading sessions.

In this book, the fifth in the *Meg and Greg* series, the learning reader begins to read some of the story text in prose rather than in speech bubbles. By this book, readers are on their seventeenth through twentieth *Meg and Greg* stories and have built the reading skills and confidence to start reading longer sections of text. The text for the learning reader continues to be decodable for a child who has learned and practiced the phonograms and concepts introduced in the first four *Meg and Greg* books (see page 9).

How does shared reading work?

Each story has several layers of text so that an adult or buddy reads the part of the story with more complex words and sentences, and the child reads the part of the story with carefully selected words and shorter sentences.

Each story has:

- *Illustration labels* for a child just starting to read or feeling overwhelmed at reading sentences. The labels are single words or short phrases and contain the story's target letters as often as possible.

- *Kid's text* for a child who has mastered the basic **consonant** sounds (including **consonant blends**), **short vowel sounds** and the **phonograms** and spellings introduced in the four previous books (Book 1: *ck, sh, ch, th*; Book 2: *nk, ng, tch, dge*; Book 3: *a-e, e-e, i-e, o-e, u-e*; Book 4: /ar/, /or/, /er/, /air/ sounds).

- *Kid's text* that always appears on the right-hand page when the book is open to a story. We also used kid's text for all story and chapter titles. As we created the stories, we bound ourselves to a set of rules that controlled the words we were "allowed" to use in the kid's text. If you're interested in these rules, they are listed on our website (megandgregbooks.com).

- *Adult or buddy reader's text*, which is the most difficult to read and always appears on the left-hand page when the book is open to a story. The buddy text uses longer sentences, a wider vocabulary and some letter combinations that the beginning reader has likely not yet learned, but it avoids very difficult words.

A child who is a more advanced reader and simply needs practice with the target concept can try reading all three layers of text in the story.

Are there any tips for buddy readers?

Yes! Try these ideas to help the child you're reading with:
- Keep the list of tricky words handy for the child to refer to when reading (see the list on page 9). Be patient! The child may need help each time they encounter a tricky word, even if they just read the word in the previous line of text.
- Before starting a story, have the child read the story title and each chapter title (in the table of contents). Ask them to predict what the story might be about.
- Before starting a story, write down a list of all the words the child might not be familiar with and review them together.
- Before you read a page of buddy text, have the child point out all the words with the target concept on the left-hand page of the open book.
- After reading each chapter, have the child speak or write one sentence that uses some of the words from the chapter. Some children might like to draw a picture.

Do the stories use "dyslexia-friendly" features?

Yes. As well as the language features throughout the story, we used design features that some people find helpful for reading:
- The font mimics as closely as possible the shapes of hand-printed letters. Children begin by learning to print letters, so we think it is important for the letter shapes to be familiar. For example, a child learns to print a not *a* and g not *g*.
- The illustration labels are printed in lowercase letters as much as possible, because children often learn to recognize and write the lowercase alphabet first.
- The spaces between lines of text and between certain letters are larger than you might see in other books.
- The kid's text is printed on shaded paper to reduce the contrast between text and paper.

Glossary

Base word: A word that can have a **prefix** or a **suffix** added to it. When a prefix or suffix is added to a base word, the word's meaning changes and a new word is formed.

Consonant: Any letter in the alphabet except for the vowels (*a, e, i, o, u*).

Consonant blend: Two or three consonants appearing at the beginning or end of a syllable. Each consonant sound is pronounced, but the sounds are so close, they seem to be blended or "glued" together. For example, *flop*, *camp* and *sprint*.

Decodable: Text that a person can read (decode) because they have learned the specific letters and sounds in the words used.

Digraph: Two letters that together make one sound, such as *ch* in *chat* and *th* in *thing*. Common digraphs are introduced in *Meg and Greg* Books 1 and 2.

Dyslexia: A term made up of *dys*, meaning "difficult," and *lexis*, meaning "word." Dyslexia tends to be used as a catchall term for a range of language-learning difficulties. These can include reading (fluency and comprehension), spelling, writing, organization skills (executive function) and even some aspects of speech.

Etymology: The study of word origins and their evolution.

Long vowel sound: The way in English that a vowel sounds when we pronounce it for a long time (longer than for **short vowel sounds**) in regular speech. For example, *bīke*, *mūte*, *rāin*, *trēe*, *gō*.

Magic *e*: A silent (not pronounced) letter *e* at the end of a word to indicate that the previous vowel is pronounced with a long sound. Consider the difference between *măd* (**short vowel sound**) and *māde* (**long vowel sound**). Magic *e* words are the focus of *Meg and Greg* Book 3.

Phonogram: Any letter or combination of letters that represents one sound. For example, the sound /k/ can be spelled with five different phonograms: c (*cat*), k (*kite*), ck (*stick*), ch (*echo*) and *que* (*antique*).

Prefix: One or more letters added to the beginning of a **base word** or a **root**. Adding a prefix creates a word with a different function or meaning. For example, adding the prefix *un-* to the base word *happy* creates the word *unhappy*.

Root: Similar to a **base word**, except a base word can stand alone in English, while a root cannot. A root can only become a word after a **prefix**, **suffix** or both have been added to it. For example, the root *-struct-* , which means "to build," cannot stand alone until a prefix like *con-* is added to it (*construct)* or a suffix like *-ure* (*structure*) or both a prefix and a suffix (*constructed*).

r-controlled vowel(s): One or two vowels that are immediately followed by the letter *r* and whose pronunciation is controlled by that *r*. Consider the difference between the pronunciation of the vowel in *băn* (**short vowel**) versus *barn* (r-controlled vowel) and in *hāil* (**long vowel**) versus *hair* (r-controlled vowel). Common r-controlled vowels are introduced in *Meg and Greg* Book 4.

Short vowel sound: The way in English that a vowel sounds when we pronounce it for a short time in regular speech. For example, *ăt, nĕt, pĭg, tŏp* and *ŭp*.

Suffix: One or more letters added to the end of a word that change the word's function or meaning. Some common suffixes are *-s, -ing* and *-er*.

Trigraph: Three letters that together make one sound, such as *tch* in *witch* and *dge* in *fudge*. Trigraphs are introduced in *Meg and Greg* Book 2.

About the authors and illustrator

Who are the authors?

Elspeth and Rowena are sisters who believe in a world where all children learn to read with confidence and have the chance to discover the pleasure of being lost in a good book.

Elspeth is a teacher certified in using the Orton Gillingham approach to teach children of all abilities to read and spell, and she especially enjoys working with children with dyslexia and other language-based learning difficulties. She lives with her husband and three children in Vancouver, British Columbia.

Rowena is a children's writer and editor living with her two children in Victoria, British Columbia.

Who is the illustrator?

Elisa is an award-winning children's book designer, illustrator and author with a passion for language and literacy. Originally from Mexico City, she lives with her husband and two children in Vancouver, British Columbia.

Acknowledgments

As with all the books in the *Meg and Greg* series, we are very grateful for the help and guidance of many different people. Ruth Linka and Andrew Wooldridge, co-publishers of Orca Book Publishers, have committed to producing another four books—numbers five through eight—in the *Meg and Greg* series. Thank you, Ruth and Andrew, for your confidence in these books and your commitment to children learning to read and practicing their newfound reading skills.

We've been especially excited to work with Vanessa McCumber, fiction editor at Orca Book Publishers, on the stories in this book. Vanessa brings the valuable perspective of a trained linguist to this project, as well as editing talent and helpful ideas about creating authentic characters and scenes. Thank you, Vanessa, for the conversations we've had while preparing this book and for your many contributions to it. Elisa also wants to thank Vanessa for her guidance in illustrating the characters of Jordan and Anka. Her perspective has been enlightening and inspiring.

We're also very grateful to work with many other members of the Orca team, including designer Ella Collier, copyeditor Vivian Sinclair, production editors Mark Grill and Renée Layberry, website specialist Michelle Simms and the entire marketing and sales departments, especially Sarah Hartley, Laura Bowman and Mya Colwell. Without all the many people involved, these books would not have the exposure they do.

The *Meg and Greg* stories come to life thanks to Elisa Gutiérrez's fabulous illustrations and design work. Thank you, Elisa, for the thought and time you put into creating engaging illustrations.

Susan Korman reviewed early drafts of the stories and gave us invaluable feedback, and Elspeth's students at Blundell Elementary in the Richmond School District test-read the stories. We are also so thankful to two young readers who spend a lot of time reading and commenting on the *Meg and Greg* stories at various stages of preparation: thank you, Rosetta de Jong and Madeleine Wilson. Last, thank you to Susan and Stan Carter, who suggested we write a pumpkin-patch story.

Thank you, readers, for joining Meg, Greg and their classmates on their adventures at Ashton Elementary. We hope you enjoyed reading the stories (and solving the clues!) as much as we enjoyed creating them!

More fun with
Meg and Greg!